HONEST, OPEN, UNAFRAID . . .

Frances Gardner Hunter embraced a thrilling new career that began at 49 when she was baptized for the second time—the most important moment in her life.

GOD IS FABULOUS! is her own true story of spiritual awakening, told with inimitable style, humor and perception. It is a book that shatters stereotypes and demands attention from all who are concerned with living life to the fullest.

p. 71 - alpha omega

page 61 -4 Spiritual laws

p. 59 - false reasons for becoming Christians

p. 33 - bathtub prayer

p. 37 - stop smoking

p. 39 stop drinking

p. 60 beach witnessing

GOD IS FABULOUS!

(The Story of an "Unsaved" Christian)

FRANCES GARDNER HUNTER

PORTAL

THE WARNER PRESS • Anderson, Indiana

GOD IS FABULOUS!

A PORTAL BOOK
Published by Pyramid Publications for Warner Press, Inc.

Sixth printing, September, 1972

ISBN 0-87162-115-0

Printed in the United States of America

PORTAL BOOKS are published by Warner Press, Inc.
1200 East 5th Street, Anderson, Indiana 46011, U.S.A.

DEDICATED TO "THE MEN IN MY LIFE"

Jesus Christ, without whom this book could never have been lived or written;

Rev. H. Peter Slagle, who heard my soul cry out, and who lovingly led me to Christ;

Ed Waxer, Area Director for the Campus Crusade for Christ, to whom I am a debtor because of the time he took in helping me learn how to win others to Christ;

Rick Strawbridge, another outstanding member of Campus Crusade for Christ, for the "young" viewpoint he gave me of Christianity; and

Gene Cotton, folk singer, who in blind faith joined with me in a vision.
     —FRANCES GARDNER HUNTER

FOREWORD

Frances Gardner Hunter is the type of Christian who if asked to pray for rain would carry an umbrella to her place of prayer. Her endless enthusiasm and immovable faith keep her ready for immediate action for the sake of Jesus Christ.

The effervescence of her personality, her refreshing honesty, and her ability to deal directly from the level of human interest, has enabled this Christian writer to prepare a book applicable to scores of people floundering in a faulty faith. The style of writing is fresh and entertaining and strikes where people act and react. The chapter on prayer is a typical example of her distinctive style. It is both amusing and enlightening.

In my work as the Crusade Director for the city-wide and area-wide crusades of the Ford Philpot

Evangelistic Association, I am constantly searching for people alive with the spirit of evangelism. Frances Gardner Hunter has proved to be such a one. In our preparation for the South Miami Crusade, she labored diligently to assist our efforts. God is using her written and personal witness to win countless souls to her "fabulous" Savior.

We of the Ford Philpot Evangelistic Association have appreciated her support and friendship, and it is with unmasked confidence that we predict beneficial inspiration for all who read the pages of this book.

JIMMY SOWDER

CONTENTS

I MEET JESUS CHRIST

I have come that they might have life, and that they might have it more abundantly.—John 10:10

For all have sinned and come short of the glory of God.—Romans 3:23

For by grace are ye saved through faith; and that not of yourselves; it is the gift of God: not of works, lest any man should boast.—Ephesians 2:8-9

THREE very short verses of Scripture, but three very important verses in my personal encounter with Jesus Christ. It is my prayer that God will allow these three verses to be very important in your life, too. Important because of what they can do for you.

I'd like to share with you how I met Jesus Christ personally. And my only reason for writing this book is a prayer that it will reach the millions of people who are "unsaved" Christians like I was. My prayer is that something in this book will come across to YOU in such a way that you will look at your own life in an honest appraisal of how you stand with Christ. I sincerely wish I had made an appraisal of myself earlier in life.

I had been a "Christian" all my life. I was raised in a church, went to church for many years, helped make the great decisions of Christianity such as "Do we have tuna fish or creamed cheese for sandwiches at the tea?" raised money for various projects, but it took me forty-eight years of life to discover "how to get the most out of life after *most* of life was gone."

Don't let this happen to you!

As I look back now, I can see that God spoke to me many times in my life, but for many years my hard-headed self-approved ability to do things myself made me buck his wonderful outstretched arms without realizing that what I was doing is probably the biggest prevailing sin in the world today—the sin of ignoring God and of compromising with Christianity—or putting it off until tomorrow because of not being ready.

I JUST DRIFTED

I had drifted away from church during the last ten years because, as I told every minister who came into my office, I could be just as good a Christian outside of church as I could be *inside*. Church honestly bored me, and my most awful thoughts came to me while sitting in church. Obviously I wasn't listening in spite of my so-called Christianity, so I began to find excuses for not attending church. After a few years I didn't even find it necessary to make excuses for not going to church.

Everyone just accepted the fact (so I thought) that I was a mighty Christian without going to church. And, anyway, after working eighteen to twenty hours a day for six days, I was entitled to sleep on Sunday, wasn't I? After all, I did have to make a living to support my children, didn't I?

The Bible says: "Thou shalt have no other gods before me." Well, *I* never did. You wouldn't either, would you? Like the god of money . . . the god of excitement . . . the god of cocktails before dinner . . . the god of cigarettes . . . the god of dancing sexy, stimulating dances for the physical thrill it gives . . . the god of clothes . . . the god of dirty jokes . . . the god of swearwords just to show people you're "cool" . . . the god of sex . . . Did you ever place any of these "gods" first in your life? Well, I'm glad you didn't, because I DID! And because I was compromising with Christianity I still went along in my little ivory palace with a slightly tarnished halo around my head.

But God has an interesting way of dealing with people like me. I shall always feel that God loved me very much because he really went out of his way to bring me into his fold. I wonder if any maverick was ever broken who kicked as hard and as long as I did.

My only son was married in 1965, and shortly before his marriage I was in an automobile accident. Little did I realize what would result from this, but three months after the accident I made the horrible discovery that I had lost the sight of my left eye.

You may think this is an awful tragedy, but I consider it the greatest blessing of my life—it took a tragedy like this to bring me to a realization of what I *didn't have in life.*

A FRIGHTENING DISCOVERY

Quite accidentally at two o'clock in the morning on a Saturday night I discovered that I could not see out of my left eye. This was a tremendous shock. I had been out for dinner and cocktails with a friend, and had started to read before I went to bed. Although I had my glasses on, I suddenly realized I couldn't see.

I was dumbfounded, but when I put my hand up to my glasses I found that the lens of the right glass had popped out. I reached into my evening bag and, sure enough, there it was! I replaced it in the frame and started reading. About twenty minutes later the startling thought struck me. Only the right lens popped out—how come I couldn't see *anything?*

Something prompted me to shut the right eye and hold it with my finger (I never could wink that eye), and to my horror I discovered that the left eye was without vision.

I promptly decided I had had too much to drink and, like Scarlett O'Hara, thought, I'll worry about that tomorrow. Tomorrow came bright and early and with it the recollection that I had had only one drink, and that I had driven home. So I made the same one-eye test I had tried the night before, and it confirmed the truth I'd tried to avoid.

I couldn't see!

On Sunday I didn't know where to reach an ophthalmologist, so I called my optometrist and told him I couldn't see. He told me to drop by and see him the next morning on my way to work. I don't believe there has ever been a day as horrible for me as Sunday, May 16, 1965. I read medical articles in every encyclopedia I could lay my hands on and before the day was over I knew I had a cataract of some kind.

That day was the birthday of the husband of a friend of mine, and I had a party for him. How I lived through it I don't know. I was smiling on the outside, but on the inside I was dying. Little did I know it then, but I actually was dying—because I think this is the event that triggered my dying to self. God was really working in my life.

During the four and a half years which preceded this accident, a certain minister had been bringing printing jobs into my office, and while I enjoyed his conversation immensely, I was deaf to his entreaties about Christianity and attending church. Still, I developed a tremendous liking for him and his theories even though I didn't practice them.

There was one thing he did, though, that didn't set right with me. He always talked about the "Lord," and I asked him one day why he didn't say "God" instead of the "Lord." I didn't tell him so, but I really thought he sounded kinda "kooky" talking about his

15

"Lord." Even though he was a young minister, I thought he was probably some kind of an old-fashioned fuddy-duddy.

GOD CLOSED IN

I bring in the fact that a particular minister prayed for me for four and a half years at this time because God was really closing in on me, even though I didn't know it.

I went to the optometrist before I opened my office the next morning and told no one what I suspected (because "I" could always handle every situation), but I did tell my head girl that I had a little eye problem.

It was several hours before I returned to the office, and everyone knew that something had happened.

And something had!

The initial examination revealed the horrible truth that a cataract had covered the lens of my eye. The optometrist took me to an ophthalmologist who said surgery was necessary. (I had already started having blinding headaches.)

Because I was so all powerful, I said "Let's get it over with, when can I go in?" This was on Monday, and I was scheduled for surgery on Friday morning.

The surgeon told me that they would remove the lens of the eye and that for four to six months I would have the eye patched, and then a contact and glasses would allow 20-20 vision.

I cried.

Because my two children have been raised without

a father, I have not allowed myself the luxury of crying very often. A mother alone has to be strong. I asked the doctor if he would allow me the privilege of being completely feminine for a few minutes and then I'd be all right.

I cried.

And I cried real hard.

I returned to my office after asking God to take good care of me, and bluntly announced what had happened. The young minister who always talked about his "Lord" was there—by coincidence? or was God working in my life?

Because I was struggling for composure, I announced that the girls could quit crying on my time since I was paying them. Then I said to the young minister, "They probably think you'll be the first one at my bedside when I come back from surgery." Now why he should be at my bedside when I had never darkened the doors of his church, and had repeatedly told him I didn't need to go to church, I'll never know —or do I?

Well, I made all the frantic preparations necessary before going to the hospital; I was due to arrive at the hospital at five o'clock on Thursday night, May 20. By seven I was there with a couple of martinis under my belt for courage.

DUSTING OFF MY BIBLE

Because I was such a devout "Christian" in times of crisis, I was shocked to discover that my maid had not put my Bible in my suitcase, and who in the world could possibly undergo surgery without the Word of God? Truthfully, I didn't even actually realize at that time that the Bible is the Word of God.

I called the friend whose husband had the birthday the Sunday before and asked her to run over to my house and bring my Bible, because she understood I simply couldn't go to surgery without reading my Bible.

I said, "Look on the top shelf of the closet, and you'll find my Bible which I love so much—it's the one dated 1924—be sure and dust it off (I hadn't read it since my last operation) and bring it to me quickly." After all, what do we all do in a crisis? We really call on God in a hurry, don't we? Maybe you don't, but I always did.

Very shortly she was there with my Bible which I opened to Psalm 23 because I think that was the only thing I had ever read in the Bible up to that time. I read, or thought I read, "The Lord is my shepherd; I shall not want."

I laid the Bible aside because I felt that was enough reading, and started to pray—even though I hadn't prayed since my last operation. Doesn't *everyone* pray in a time of crisis?

I really prayed!

I said, "Oh, God, don't let the operation hurt tomorrow. I can stand anything, but don't let it hurt when they operate on my eye." I did what we all do—I really ignored God during good times, and then ran screaming for help when the tide went against me!

I tried to recall the words I had read: "The Lord is my shepherd; I shall not want." But I guess what I really did was to pick up my Bible again and look to see what it actually said, and I think what I saw that night was the handwriting of God as he said, "Frances Gardner, I LOVE YOU." Of all the people in the world, God said he loved *me*.

I think in one world-shattering moment I got a glimpse of what my life had been—a constant, "Oh, God, *YOU* do this for me!" And never a thought as to what I could do for him.

I didn't know what I was doing really, but in that moment I said, "God, I take back that prayer, and I don't care how much it hurts tomorrow, but I promise You this. When I get out of this hospital, I will spend the rest of my life seeing what I can do for Jesus Christ, and not what he can do for me."

Little do we realize what we say in times like this, and how much truth is spoken during trials and tribulations.

I returned from surgery the next morning at about eleven, and there, standing by my bed, was the young minister who served his "Lord." I was so doped up I didn't make much sense, but one sentence came out. "I'm going to visit your church when I get out of this hospital." God knew that one of his sheep was lost and he had sent a shepherd to find her and bring her into the fold.

My recovery was excellent, and in just ten days I returned to work wearing all sorts of fancy eye patches. I had one for every dress I owned. Even though I wore a broad smile on the outside, I had discovered that something was missing from my life. This kind of an operation destroys your depth perception

19

... I couldn't drive my car ... I couldn't get my food into my mouth without spilling it all over me. It can be a frustrating item with a patch over your eye twenty-four hours a day!

GOING TO CHURCH

But I remembered what I had promised God in the hospital, and before my operation was two weeks old, I went to church. I was so weak I could hardly make it, but somewhere God had given me a taste of the living water and it started a compelling desire for MORE ... MORE ... MORE.

I didn't know it, but it was Communion Sunday and because the minister said it was open to all Christians, I certainly participated. What a counterfeit Christian I was! And then I heard an unusual sermon. *And it was an unusual sermon because I met Jesus Christ personally for the first time.* It was not a gentle meeting—I ran head on into Jesus Christ and for many months it was a question of who had the hardest head.

What an encounter! For the first time in my life I realized I was *not* a Christian. I certainly didn't admit it to anyone—not even myself! What a horrible discovery to make when you're forty-eight years old. I remember thinking, I can't let God know about this, because he thinks I'm a Christian. Oh, foolish woman, God knew it all the time. I was so confused and in such a state of shock to even *think* that I might not be a Christian, that I didn't know what to do.

I was so shook up that Sunday I didn't even listen

completely, but something was said about Jesus standing at the door of your heart, knocking, and asking you to open the door. (Revelation 3:20: "I stand at the door and knock; if any one hears my voice and opens the door, *I will come in to him. . . .*") But then the minister said something about asking for forgiveness of your sins. Well, I thought that bit about the forgiveness of your sins was about the most stupid thing I had ever heard, because in my opinion I *was absolutely without sin.* After all, wasn't I donating printing jobs to churches, and wasn't I being a real good little "do bee"?

The Bible says, "All have sinned and come short of the glory of God." But I didn't know that because I had never read that much of the Bible.

However, the compelling force in my life had begun, a force so strong and so powerful that *nothing* was to stand in the way of total commitment. The compelling force that drove me was a desire to see that I knew everything there was to know about this man Jesus Christ, and a desire to see that everyone knew him personally as I did. However, even though I did know him personally, I had not completely accepted all the things he said in the Bible.

I drove every Christian crazy because I wanted to know how to "recruit" for Christ. I read the Bible with a complete fanaticism as though it wasn't going to be there the next day. In two years I read the New Testament fourteen times in many different translations.

I went to church every Sunday morning and was so spiritually charged up—but completely miserable during the altar call week after week—that it seemed to me my soul was absolutely torn out of my body.

I begged . . . I pleaded . . . I cried . . . Sunday after Sunday, and said, "God, You know I want to be a totally dedicated Christian—what's the matter with YOU? Why don't you take ALL of me?" You see, I *knew* I was not a totally dedicated Christian.

This went on Sunday after Sunday for months and months. I couldn't wait to go to church, and I couldn't wait to get home afterwards because I was so torn up inside, and because I never took along enough Kleenex to wipe my tears. The Bible says, "Ye must be born again." How stupid can some of us be? Over and over again I asked God what was the matter with HIM.

By Thanksgiving of 1965, God had restored my left eye to 20-20 vision with the help of a contact and glasses, and I went to church very grateful for what he had done for me. As I sat there and listened to the sermon about thanking the Lord for what he had done for us, God continued to deal harshly with me, but only because of his great love and because the Holy Spirit was really working on me to show me the way.

SEEING MYSELF

When the sermon was over, I didn't dare look down because I was afraid to! I knew I didn't have a stitch of clothes on! Do you know what it's like to be sitting in church absolutely naked? It's horrible. God had stripped me of my outer clothing to show me exactly what I was and all I could say was, "What's the mat-

22

ter with YOU, God, you know I want to be dedicated 100 percent."

I think at least ten times every day I asked Christ to come into my life. I visually imagined the kind of a door my heart had. I knew which way it opened, and each time I would say, "I don't think You're in there, so I'll ask You again just in case." My faith was *really great*! The Bible says, "For by grace are ye saved through *faith.*" I didn't even have enough faith to know that Jesus does what he says he will. He says if you will open the door, he will come in. But over and over I kept asking him to come in. His love and grace and mercy must be tremendous that he could still keep loving someone like me, who doubted so much and who still had not found the secret of being a Christian.

And then one day I was standing in church singing a song, and God reminded me of SIN in my life. I honestly believe this was a greater shock to me than discovering I wasn't a Christian. All of a sudden Frances Gardner crumbled into nothing and died to self and was born again, because for the first time I said, "O God, what's the matter with ME? And in the loving, wonderful way that God has, he nudged me and said, "Remember?" Horrified, I said, "You knew that all along," . . . and then my whole life flashed before me and I begged forgiveness for my sins.

Someone had asked me once when I was "saved." I had answered, "Saved from what?" Finally I realized that I had been saved from sin, a thing I had refused to admit that I had ever committed, even though the Bible says, "ALL have sinned and come short of the glory of God." It also says, "The wages of sin are death." I had been spiritually dead all these years because I *could not admit sin.*

And *only then,* because finally I had received God's forgiveness for my sins, could I ask Christ to live his life through me, and be the Lord of my life. At last I understood what the "Lord" meant.

But, interestingly enough, when salvation came, it came so quietly I don't even know the date. No lightning . . . no thunder . . . just peace and calm.

CHAPTER 2

I FIND THE HOLY SPIRIT

When he, the Spirit of truth, is come, he will guide you into all truth.—John 16:13

Be filled with the Spirit.—Ephesians 5:18

If we live in the Spirit, let us also walk in the Spirit.—Galatians 5:25

IT'S A marvelous thing that God doesn't reveal all of his Kingdom to us at one time—I doubt if we could stand it in one big dose. Maybe that is why he gives us only a little glimpse of truth at a time, because each tiny glimpse is so overwhelming and so overpowering that a massive dose might be fatal.

Once the compelling force in my life had begun, everything in my life was pointed in one direction only—all I could think of was Jesus Christ, the love of my life! Everything else fell by the wayside and was completely secondary to this Man who had changed my entire being—my entire way of life—my entire way of thinking—my entire reason for living!

But I still had such a long way to go—and I still do. And then one day I was setting some type for a job which mentioned a desire to be filled with the "Holy Spirit."

My pastor always seems to drop by the office just when some spiritual crisis arises—or does the Lord send him there? I couldn't possibly imagine what being filled with the Holy Spirit meant, so when he came in to pick up some work, I just asked him point blank, "What does it mean to be filled with the Holy Spirit?" And I hope in reading this you will remember that most of my life I had gone to church and Sunday school, but I had never heard of the power of the Holy Spirit.

He said, "When you are born again and God forgives your sins, you become a clean vessel which the Holy Spirit can fill with power for your Christian life." This made no sense to me, and I wondered for a minute if he was kidding me. I couldn't understand what in the world the Holy Spirit was.

Then I did what I always do when I discover something new in Christianity. I ran for the Bible and looked up every reference to the Holy Spirit. I went to the Bible store and bought every little tract and book which I could find concerning the Holy Spirit. Also, about this time our Bible Study Class began studying the Holy Spirit, and I discovered that in Ephesians we are commanded to be filled with the Holy Spirit.

It's amazing what happens to your life when the Holy Spirit comes in. He brings a power unbelievable to a nonbeliever.

THE "ZING" OF CHRISTIANITY

The ability to witness and to transmit the fact of God's love is there—the ability to win others to Christ becomes a reality—the ability to follow God's will becomes a routine thing. In other words, the Holy Spirit is the "zing" of Christianity.

Each time I have sat down to write on this book I have asked God to fill me afresh with his Holy Spirit, and I have asked the Holy Spirit to use my brains and my fingers on the typewriter to bring this story to life so that anyone who might read it will feel the vibrant living thing that Christianity is. A personal relationship with Jesus Christ is the only thing in the world that's worthwhile, for the Bible says: "Seek ye *first* the kingdom of God."

As I read that recently I wondered what comes second. I have never found time to do anything but "seek ye *first*," because the seeking and the searching is a lifetime proposition to me at any rate, and I doubt if there will ever be time to seek anything else.

Not only that, the Bible says the fruit of the Spirit is love, joy, peace, patience, kindness, goodness, faithfulness, gentleness, self-control. When you are filled with the Holy Spirit, you have ALL this (and heaven, too), and with all the wonderful blessings of his Holy Spirit, how could you possibly want for anything except more of the wonderful promises of God?

A SPECIAL QUALITY

There is a special quality to those who are filled with the Holy Spirit. He imparts a special vibrance, a special "come-alive" warmth to an individual, a special radiance, a special outgoing Christian love which is distinguishable in a room, on a street, on a stage, or anywhere an individual happens to be. The defeated Christians today—and there are many, many of them —are defeated because they do not ask to be filled with the Holy Spirit.

The Holy Spirit gives freedom from the things of the world . . . the Holy Spirit brings every single part of you, both physical and mental, into an exciting relationship with Jesus Christ! Without the Holy Spirit you will fail.

If you want to be a failure in Christianity, don't ask to be filled with the Holy Spirit. If you want to be an automobile that runs out of gas and can never run again, don't ask for a refilling of the Holy Spirit. If you want to lead a useless life, don't ask to be filled with the Holy Spirit.

BUT if you want ACTION in your life, ask right now to be filled with the Holy Spirit. And get the debris out of the road, because action is what you'll get!

CHAPTER 3

I LEARN TO PRAY ...
IN THE BATHTUB

Whatever you ask in prayer, you will receive, if you have faith.—Matthew 21:22, RSV

ONCE the "bug" of Christianity had really bitten me, I couldn't read enough, study enough, buy enough inspirational books, pray enough, or accomplish enough of anything I wanted to do.

UNABLE TO PRAY

The biggest stumbling block in my Christian life, however, seemed to be my inability to pray out loud. I could send up all kinds of prayers to God in silence, by just thinking, but I discovered I just couldn't open my mouth and pray out loud.

At my age it's difficult to admit you don't know how to pray, but I do remember telling my pastor if he ever called on me to say a public prayer he wouldn't get a prayer, but a big "thud" which would be me fainting dead away.

I went to a study group on prayer and found myself learning how to pray to God, in the name of Jesus Christ, and through his Holy Spirit, and after what must have been months, I finally was called on to say a benediction. My throat tightened up, my heart pounded so loud I knew everyone could hear it, and if I had opened my eyes I know I could have seen it beating. I finally struggled through a magnificent prayer which consisted of three words, "Thank You, Lord."

And then I cried.

I went home that night and wondered why I couldn't pray, and then I felt that I had really let God down. The wonderful God of Love who answers prayers, the God who had never let me down, and I couldn't even talk to him out loud!

After I got home that night I asked God to teach me how to pray. I asked him to fill me so full of his Holy Spirit that I would be just running over with prayer. And I got into the bathtub. Something about the soothing quality of water (or bubble bath) made me decide this was the perfect place to learn how to pray and, anyway, nobody could hear me.

I have prayed more prayers in my bathtub than probably any other single place. The quietness and the fact that my family never disturbs me makes the bathtub a perfect place to pray.

For the next six months I was probably the most scrubbed, bathed woman in Florida. As I discovered how to pray, a new dimension came into my life, and not only did I discover *how* to pray, I discovered how wonderful it is to pray, and how easy it is to pray and keep in constant communion with our heavenly Father.

There is one thing I would like to caution the reader about, however, in connection with learning to pray in the bathtub.

In my energetic urge for Christianity, and the surge for maturity, the Lord decided to use me as a soul winner. I had no problem witnessing about what Christ could do in a life because of what he had done in mine, and because I always asked the Lord to fill me with his Holy Spirit and to speak through me, many individuals have been led to Christ. But I discovered that when they accepted Christ, the next step was to ask them to pray a prayer of repentance, and I couldn't help because the only place I could pray was in the bathtub!

I often wondered what some new Christian would have thought if I had said, "Would you mind jumping into the bathtub because that's the only place I can pray."

I never did, though, and I finally did learn how to pray publicly.

PRAYER TIMES

There are many kinds of prayer times. There is the time when it's just "time to pray." I'm not real crazy about this kind because I like to pray when I feel like

31

prayer . . . either because I feel very strongly on some subject or because of some tremendous need in my own life or the life of another.

My children always ask me to say the blessing at the supper table because they know that's when they get to find out about all the fabulous things that happened during the day, and as a result our house has the most unusual "grace" period imaginable. Actually, this is our devotional time because it's the only time we are all together, and this is when we bare our hearts and our innermost thoughts. The prayers that have been answered as the result of this are unbelievable.

Once in a while we do remember to ask that the food bless our bodies as we present them a living sacrifice, holy, and acceptable to God. Dinners have become cold upon occasion when everyone felt led to pray, but I have never had a complaint about a cold dinner caused by warm prayers!

Probably the greatest miracle in my life occurred because of prayer—not just lukewarm prayer, but fervent prayer—but this is a separate story in itself.

Learning how to talk to God can be a fabulous experience, if you will let it. And talking to God can make your entire life fabulous.

I have a little prayer which I send up to God every morning when I wake up, but let me caution you—*don't say it unless you mean it!* Before I open my eyes in the morning I say, "Well, Lord, what fabulous things are we going to do today?"

And do you know what? Every day is *fabulous!*

Last Thanksgiving I went to Lakeland, Florida, to

be a counselor at the state youth convention. By the time I returned, I was exhausted. We had a death in our church, had a special guest the morning we returned, and went to church dedication service that afternoon, so I was completely ground down. On Monday morning I said, "God, do You think we could have a dumb, dull, stupid day because I'm so tired?"

And do you know what?

I had a real dumb, dull stupid day! But by Tuesday morning there I was back again saying, "What fabulous things are we going to do today?"

I would like to challenge each of you who read these pages to ask God what fabulous thing he's going to do with you today.

But remember, . . . if you don't have the courage to accept his fabulous offerings, don't pray.

CHAPTER 4

"JUST AS I AM"

I WONDER how many people have felt the call to come to Christ as the famous song "Just As I Am" was being sung? One of the most misunderstood phases of Christianity is the state of our being when we accept Christ. Having worked with many as they were led to Christ in various ways, probably the biggest single reason given for not wanting to accept Christ at a particular time is, "I've got to get rid of some bad habits first."

Oh, foolish sinner, God wants each and every one of us "just as we are." Even though my Christian experience does not span many years, it spans a lot of people, and I have never yet met one who by himself "got rid of some bad habits."

The most amazing thing about Christianity is that there is only one thing a human has to do, and that is to surrender or yield his life totally to Christ . . . of course, this is the most difficult thing in the world to do, and something many people fail to accomplish.

In this particular phase of my life, I believe God dealt very kindly with me. In most things I had to put up a fight and struggle, but I was so stupid I really didn't think there was anything wrong with any phase of my life now that I was a Christian.

I was a five-pack-a-day chain smoker and had lighted cigarettes laying all over ashtrays in my office, in my house, in my car, everywhere. I often wonder if I must not have smelled like a most unfeminine furnace all the time.

I had begun a lot of work with the youth in the church, and my home was running over with them constantly. I always drank my nightly martini and smoked incessantly in front of all of them, because I felt there was nothing wrong with this. But as the weeks and months went on, a verse in the Bible kept coming to my mind: "I appeal to you therefore, brethren, by the mercies of God, to present your bodies as a living sacrifice, holy and acceptable to God" (Romans 12:1, RSV).

I FELT UNCOMFORTABLE

The Holy Spirit had begun his work again of convicting me because all of a sudden I began to feel uncomfortable smoking in front of my pastor (who had never commented on this situation). I discovered I could no longer keep chain-smoking when he came into the office, and then finally I couldn't even contin-

ue smoking the lighted cigarette in fron
to let it burn itself out because su~~bconsciously~~ I
began to feel that smoking was keeping me from pre-
senting my body as a "living sacrifice, holy and acceptable to God."

I had stopped smoking twice before in my life, after
the birth of both of my children, but each time I had
broken out in a horrible skin rash which about drove
me out of my mind, and which disappeared both
times *after* I started smoking again, so I always knew
I would smoke myself right into my grave because I
just couldn't quit smoking.

And how right I was! *I* couldn't quit smoking, and *I*
never did. But one night as I was working late, my
pastor dropped by with the church bulletin on his
round of evening calls. I had just bought a carton of
cigarettes and was smoking the first one. Sitting there
the thought came to me, *What* controls my life—or
Who controls my life? Did Christ actually control my
life as I thought, or did a miserable piece of tobacco
control my life? I was smoking four cartons a week,
and couldn't even buy them all at the same store because the employees would comment, "You just
bought a carton." I was a "cigaretteholic" and I would
make all kinds of excuses as to why I was out of cigarettes so fast, always saying that I didn't smoke that
many. This addiction is the same as that of an alco-
holic or a dope fiend.

As my pastor walked in, I said, "I'd quit this stinking habit if I thought I wouldn't break out in a rash."

He simply pointed a finger to heaven and said,
"Why don't you ask Him to help you?"

I said: "For a stinking little thing like cigarettes?"

He said: "For a stinking little thing like cigarettes!" And he left.

I sat there watching the smoke curl up and said, "God, You know that I can't quit. If I try, I'll be tortured and tormented and miserable and then I'll break out in a nervous rash, but if You don't think I'm a good example to young people, would You do it for me?"

GOD HELPED ME

I have never smoked another cigarette, nor have I ever had a desire for one. But you see, *I* never quit, so therefore I couldn't have a desire for something *I* hadn't given up. (And I didn't break out in a rash, either!)

I secretly felt very smug about the whole thing in the beginning because it had been no effort on my part, but this was only because of a lack of understanding on my part. I kept an unopened pack of cigarettes on my nightstand and every night as I flipped into bed I would say to the cigarettes: "See how smart *I* am. *I* quit smoking," and then I went to bed feeling completely righteous. About three months later as I jumped into bed the realization struck me that if Christ was living my life *I* had nothing to do with smoking because I had been "crucified with Christ; it is no longer *I* who live, but Christ who lives in me" (Galatians 2:20, RSV).

I threw the pack of cigarettes into the wastebasket.

who can enjoy a martini without a cigarette?

Martinis had never been a problem with ᵣ cause the grace of God saw to it that I ha⏑ ⏑⏑ierance for alcohol. Even though I did enjoy one martini, I never could go much beyond the first one, but I guess I knew that my Christian witness would suffer as long as I had a martini in my hand—but how do you tell your old friends that you "don't drink anymore"?

Well, the Lord settled that one for me, too. I went to a friend's house whose husband thought I had flipped my wig and become a "religious fanatic." He insisted that I had to take a martini because surely I hadn't "gone so far that I couldn't enjoy getting a little high."

I felt like I was backed into a corner and didn't have the courage to fight. The first time you say "I don't drink" is the *only* time it's hard, but it really is hard to say that first time! Probably because I was still partly a spiritual chicken I cried out again for Christ to do something for me.

And he did!

As I was debating in my own mind about whether to pick the drink up and just hold it, or make the brazen statement that I didn't drink, I looked at the glass. . . . Only I didn't see the glass. All I saw was a snake! And the Person who had changed my life so drastically had made another change only because I had yielded my all to him.

No one ever offered me a martini again. Somehow they knew without my ever saying anything that I just didn't drink anymore. I didn't HAVE to drink anymore because I had only to remember and recall the presence of God to be lifted up to the highest plane, and how could anyone ever be downhearted or sad when in his presence?

When the Christmas season came the first year after my conversion, many of my friends did not invite me to the usual Christmas parties because I "had really changed." By the second year they were beginning to realize this was not a temporary thing, but that something had really happened in my life. Many of my friends joined in the same walk, and many watched my life in amazement, but could not enter the same narrow gate. However, they invited me to their parties the second year with the reminder, "We'll have Coke for you," or, "You can drink your eggnog plain."

I don't enjoy going to cocktail parties anymore because the conversation is so inane and so shallow, so I go only on rare occasions. And it amazes me to see what happens. All of a sudden everyone is asking me questions, and the highball glasses are sitting on the tables and the drinks are going flat because the ice cubes are melting in them.

A friend took a picture behind my back at a party one night and it was real interesting . . . the only person with a glass in his hand was me! And the expressions on their faces as they listened to my testimony told a very interesting story.

LOOKING FOR KICKS

I think people who drink are looking for "kicks" and are trying to get themselves on a higher plane than they are during an average day, and so they resort to the artificial stimulation of alcohol to give them "kicks." If only they realized the truth of the verse in Ephesians: "And do not get drunk with wine, for that is debauchery; but be filled with the Spirit" (5:18, RSV), they would find that a spiritual "kick" is a permanent state of being—a way of life if you please—that replaces any and all of the worldly things in a heavenly manner.

My heart cries out daily because of those who are so blind they cannot see the Life that wins. Even though they are amazed at the change which has come because I asked Christ to live his life through me, they realize that the changes were made because he was willing to accept me "Just As I Am," and today the story is turned around because they, too, accept me "Just As I Am." But what a difference in the two meanings! As the wonderful words of Paul say in Philippians 1:21: "For me to *live* is Christ, and to die is gain," and by dying to self I have really learned to live.

And no one ever asks me to smoke a cigarette or drink a martini anymore.

CHAPTER 5

I AM BAPTIZED

I WAS "sprinkled" when I was a little girl. I don't even remember exactly when it was nor can I find the baptismal certificate, but during the many years I wore my tarnished halo as a bonafide "counterfeit Christian," I knew that I had been "baptized."

After my personal encounter with Jesus Christ, one day in church came the announcement that all those who had been "saved" would be baptized by request in four weeks, and then we heard a sermon on "Why Baptism by Immersion."

For some reason or other, from my early childhood on I remember having an aversion to denominations that believed in "dunking" people. I put this in the same category as the word "saved," and I definitely shied away from anything that sounded like immersion. However, the Holy Spirit took care of this problem for me beautifully, and again God dealt harshly with me because of my own stubbornness.

Something put doubt into my mind as to whether I had actually been baptized or not. I read all the Scriptural references I could find, and nothing seemed to satisfy me. I talked to my pastor, assuring him that I had been baptized, and he laid the decision right back in my lap. Kindly and gently, but firmly, he said, "You'll have to make your own decision, Frances." I decided right then that he should be more positive about things like this so that he could tell people whether they should be rebaptized or not. But how smart he was . . . he knew the decision had to be my very own, and not something someone talked me into doing.

I was real busy lining up all my spiritual children for the big event, but in the back of my own mind was the ever-present thought of my own baptism.

Our church didn't have a baptismal pool and since I live in Florida where many people have swimming pools, the baptizing is often done in such pools. I couldn't help but feel this was the living end to put on an old white choir robe and walk into a friend's pool and get your hairdo ruined when I *knew* I had been baptized many years ago. And, anyway, I was forty-nine years old, and it's ridiculous to be baptized with a bunch of teen-agers when you're that old.

But God continued to deal with me, and I could think of nothing else. I kept thinking I heard the words over and over, "You've got too much pride to be baptized, don't you?" And again I talked and talked to God, trying to talk him out of being baptized publicly at my age.

But it doesn't pay to argue with God. I always win when I do, but I only win because I give in to him. With me the only way an argument with God can possibly end is for him to have his way in my life.

I finally went to my minister and announced I wanted to be baptized along with my daughter because I knew where I was going, and while I didn't feel the Bible said anything about failure to be baptized keeping you from eternal life, I wasn't going to take any chances. When I sat in his office after church one night and told him this, I felt a thousand-pound weight removed from my chest.

The Sunday came when we were all to be baptized, and we were to be at the swimming pool for a public service at three o'clock that afternoon. A number of the teens were over at my house; as we dressed for the service, I felt the presence of God so strongly I knew I had obeyed him with my decision to be baptized.

I felt I would burst—my heart actually seemed to beat as though it would break out of my chest. I tried to remain calm because some people have emotional reactions to certain things, and others don't, and I don't feel the degree of your Christianity depends on the emotional feelings you have. I knew that no one noticed anything unusual about the way I felt until one of the boys said, "How come you have your dress on backwards?"

I had put on my bathing suit and slipped a shift

over it, and in my utter *calm* I had put the dress on backwards.

It was a short drive to the swimming pool and when we arrived I was shocked to find such a large crowd there. The minister walked into the pool and one by one baptized the young people. I have a vague recollection of being next to the last, or last, I'm not sure which because something really happened to me that day.

A man in our congregation led me into the water (my problem with my second eye had started and was getting very serious, so seeing was a real problem for me). I remember stretching out my hand to reach the minister because I couldn't see anything without my glasses on—and I don't remember anything else. There is a very vague recollection of him asking me if I had accepted Jesus Christ as my Savior and Lord, and I think I said, "You *know* I have."

I must have been immersed, but I don't remember it except that I was soaking wet; he must have called out my name, but I didn't hear it; he must have walked me to the steps because I couldn't see to walk by myself; someone must have helped me from the pool, but I don't remember anything except the rushing of waters over my face. Before they closed over me, my soul went right straight into the ever-loving outstretched arms of God.

It seems to me we sang "Thank You, Lord, for *saving* my soul," but it was all hazy. My usual talkative self had been awed and silenced by the overpowering presence of God. I couldn't wait to get away—all I wanted to do was go home and read my Bible. I felt

I Am Baptized

I would scream if anyone talked to me because I didn't want to ever break the spell of the presence of God. I went home, grabbed my Bible, and with the arms of God wrapped tightly around me, I read his wonderful words all afternoon.

I think baptism is the thing that sealed me and bound me forever.

CHAPTER 6

I LEARN TO WITNESS

WHEN Christ came into my life, he opened my mouth, and I haven't shut it yet! And I pray that I never will. I had the most burning desire to share what had happened to me with everyone I met, and the Lord who always honors a sincere heart crossed my path with another of the "men in my life."

One day a young man walked into my office and when I looked up from my desk at him to ask him if I could help him, all I could see were the eyes of Christ looking at me from a different face than I expected. I quickly decided that Christianity had got the best of me, and I was really imagining things, until he opened his mouth and said, "I'm Ed Waxer of the Campus Crusade for Christ."

Somehow in the way we never question, God's Holy Spirit had told me here was a brother in Christ, before I ever knew who he was. I am a debtor of Ed Waxer, a Christian of Jewish background, for the time he has taken to help me mature as a Christian.

As I look back on it now, he must have thought I was a batty old lady, but he realized that the drive and the compelling force which possessed me was a dedication to Christ. I nagged and nagged and pleaded and begged, "Please teach me how to 'recruit.'" What I really meant was "Teach me how to lead others to Christ," but in my unchristian jargon I didn't know what to call it except recruiting for God's army. Poor Ed was so busy trying to activate the campus program down here, he really didn't have time, but finally he promised he would come over to my house and teach me how to "recruit."

I was almost hysterical. He had told me I could invite three other people from the church, but somehow I invited seven, and I made the eighth person. Ed brought another staff member of Campus Crusade and we divided into two groups to learn how to "recruit."

FOUR SPIRITUAL LAWS

Ed showed us how they present the "Four Spiritual Laws" which the Campus Crusade for Christ uses internationally. This is a simplified presentation of the plan of salvation. Ed carefully explained every step and assured us it would work and turn our church upside down if we would try it.

I had been literally dragging people to church with me because I had read that Paul said, "I have become all things to all men, that I might by all means save some" (1 Corinthians 9:22, RSV). I felt that everyone in the whole city of Miami simply had to go to church and hear the claims of Christ, but to win someone to Christ . . . that was something else.

I studied the Four Spiritual Laws and read and reread them. Our church formed a "GO" Committee. During a meeting the minister gave out "GO" cards or calls we were to make and present the four spiritual laws.

A church friend and I (we are now known as the GO-GO girls) made a promise to God that before the week was over we would go and make a call and present the Four Spiritual Laws.

Monday came and I called and said, "Barb, I'm so busy at the office I've got to work tonight. Can we call it off tonight?"

Barb said that was all right with her, we would go the next night. The next night she called me with some phony excuse. . . . And the next night was the midweek service, so neither of us had to make up a phony excuse. . . . Then the next night I called her and gave her a phony excuse. And on Friday she called me because she was having company. . . . And we both decided Saturday would be a bad time to go.

AND ALL OF A SUDDEN IT WAS SUNDAY!

And we had promised God we would make a call before the "GO" meeting at 6:00 p.m. on Sunday.

After church on Sunday morning, I called Barbara and said, "We pledged—and we just *have* to do it."

And she agreed.

Well, I tried to think of everything to make us so

late we couldn't possibly make a "GO" call on anyone because I was SCARED. I had temporarily forgotten the Bible says: "But you shall receive *power* when the Holy Spirit has come upon you; and you shall be my witnesses in Jerusalem and in all Judea and Samaria and to the end of the earth" (Acts 1:8, RSV).

TIME WAS RUNNING OUT

I picked Barb up at five o'clock, and we knew that time was running out, but even so we remembered a friend in the hospital who maybe we ought to go and see. But after a hurried conference, we didn't, because we had made a covenant with God, and we knew we had to keep it.

We went to the house assigned to us and I did some of the fastest praying in my life—but some of the most stupid. I prayed: "Dear God, please don't let anyone be home. We just can't do this. Please . . . please." As we got closer I pleaded, begged, cried, rebelled, and asked him to see that no one was home.

And then I saw a light in the house.

. . . And then I saw that the door was open.

I reminded God that maybe she was out and had just left the door open and could I please turn around? Relentlessly, God said, "GO."

Both Barb and I nearly fainted when a woman came to the door. We had previously decided that Barb was going to read the Four Spiritual Laws because she had been a Christian longer than I had; so we walked in and I honestly have no idea what we said, but before long Barb was reading the Four Spiritual Laws.

Four very simple, but beautiful laws, all backed up with the proper Scripture.

No. 1 merely states that God loves you and has a plan for your life.

(I won't argue with that.)

No. 2 states that "all have sinned and come short of the glory of God."

(I won't argue with that.)

No. 3 states that "Jesus Christ is God's only provision for man's sin."

(I won't argue with that.)

No. 4 states: "I stand at the door and knock. If any man hear my voice and open the door, I will come in to him."

(I won't argue with that either.)

And then you ask the person you've been talking to if he would like to invite Christ to come into his life.

Barb asked the woman if she would like to invite Christ into her life. And she said Yes.

Barb and I both felt as though we had been struck with lightning!

We had kept our covenant with God, but had forgotten that he would be with us, so we were not prepared for success. Oh, how pathetic it is when we don't put faith in God's promises.

Barb looked at me, and I looked at her, and we both thought, She's kidding. So Barb asked her again and when she said Yes again, we looked at each other and in the same instant we realized how little was our faith. God has never let me down, but I often wonder how many times I have let him down.

We came to our senses then, and Barb said the only thing either of us could think of to say: "Let's pray." She did, and we felt the presence of the Holy Spirit as he is always felt when someone is led to Christ.

We said our "good-byes" with tears in our eyes because this had been a tremendous experience for all of us. As we went down to the car, we thanked our Lord for his tender, loving care which had directed two sincere women who didn't know what they were doing, but knew what they wanted to do.

We flew back to the church and practically tore our pastor apart because we were so excited because we had led our first person to Christ. We followed this up two nights later with another thrilling win for Christ, and I did the talking that time.

Since then the Lord has blessed Barb and me many times, but I often wonder if any convert will ever do for us what the first one did.

CHAPTER 7

I FIND WITNESSING IS EXCITING

THERE is no thrill in the world which compares with leading someone to Christ! What happens in your own life when you have "faced" a person with Jesus Christ and he has accepted Him is indescribable.

Do let me give you the only hint I can concerning witnessing: Don't ever try to do it on your own, or you'll fail! As Barb and I went on "GO" calls, we never talked in the car, but prayed, and asked God to fill us with his Holy Spirit and let the words that were to come from our lips be his words, and not ours. Only when you are yielded to his Holy Spirit can you be an effective witness.

Our young people wanted to learn how to win others to Christ, so one night after a midweek service we held a training class. The pastor was called out, so he asked me to take over and show the young people how to present the Four Spiritual Laws.

I presented them as I would in anyone's home, and as I got to the fourth law concerning Christ's invitation, I realized I was talking to a group made up of about 50 percent non-Christians. I stormed the gates of heaven with prayer asking God's guidance, because how could these young people be successfully taught to be soul winners when they were not Christians?

God's very presence was in the room that night as he touched the young people one by one and they opened the doors of their hearts to invite Christ in. And I felt my "cup run over" because my physical daughter was now also my spiritual daughter, for she, too, accepted Christ.

ON THE BEACH

The young people wanted to win others to Christ after seeing a film entitled "Bal Week" which showed Campus Crusaders witnessing on the beaches. Two carloads of us went to a local beach one Sunday afternoon; the young people knew they could really turn Miami upside down by holding an evangelistic movement on the beaches. Barb and I went and sat down to await results and give them spiritual encouragement.

Satan always comes in when he feels Christians maturing, so he planted F-E-A-R into them. About ten youth walked around the beach where hundreds of people were sitting; then they came back and reported, "There isn't anyone we can witness to."

Once the witnessing bug has bitten you, it is impossible to keep still, and I was really champing at the bit. I could see potential in every group singing, swimming, swinging, or what have you; so they said, "All right, *you* do it if you think it's so easy."

I had better explain to the reader right now that I am not a movie star type. In the first place my age is against me for purposes of beauty (but for enjoyment of life, it's really *with* me!). In the second place I would say I'm approximately twice the size of the average woman, so this doesn't add to my physical charms. (It's a blessing, though, when people want to cry on your shoulder to have a big enough shoulder to cry on!) But God made me and he loves me, and so this must be the way he wants me. Who am I to complain?

It's essential when in Rome to do as Romans do, so before leaving home I put on a bathing suit, carefully covering it with a shift. I kicked off my shoes and walked across the sand to the first group I saw.

And what a group! They all were nineteen to twenty-two years old. Real beatniks! Beards, bikinis, liquor, the whole bit. I said, "Lord, you'd better handle this all the way or I'm sunk."

I walked up, sat down between two of the young men, and said, "Would you good-looking young men mind if an old lady sits down with you?"

I hope you will remember that I have been in business for ten years and most people consider me successful, reliable, dependable, and so forth. And the answer of this beatnik group could have knocked me off my feet had I not asked God to do the job for me.

"What are you, some kind of fruit?"

I remembered the old saying, "If you can't beat

'em, join 'em." So I said, "Yes, and if you don't believe it, you can ask my twenty-year-old son. But he'll tell you I'm a square pushed out, or a cube, which is even worse. . . . Now, boys, do we talk your language, or mine?"

Silence.

I told them I was taking a religious survey and would appreciate their answering some questions. They agreed to answer the questions, but they had decided to roast me like a pig on a spit.

I asked them a few introductory questions about their plans for the future, and their nondescript answers indicated that they were all going to be bums. They had no plan for their lives. I said I thought this was fabulous, because since they had no plan, I knew they'd be interested in knowing that God has a plan for them.

One finally admitted that he was going to be a surfer and he really perked up when I told him I was personally acquainted with the world's greatest surfer. "Jesus Christ," I said, "because he didn't need a surfboard; he just walked on the water."

This made an impression on them, and they promptly asked me to go to an Ale House with them.

I declined.

Next, I asked them whom they knew the most about, Mohammed, Buddha, or Jesus Christ. They all got real smart-alecky and answered, "Mohammed. Doesn't everybody?" One thing to remember during a survey—don't reply to or comment on any answer regardless of your personal feelings.

At this point I gave a little testimony on my own

58

life and one young fellow said, "Put me down for Jesus Christ, Ma'am."

The Holy Spirit had come to walk on the beach.

I had been sitting there wondering what I was doing on the beach when I hate the sand, the salt, the water, the breeze, and so on. Then I remembered how Jesus witnessed on the shores of Galilee, and I decided if it was good enough for him, it was certainly good enough for me. And anyway, if he was living his life through me, who was sitting on the beach?

The transition question had been answered, so I asked them how a person becomes a Christian. At this point three others joined the group, so I now had seven. The newcomers joined not because of a personal invitation from me, but because the original four grabbed them into the group.

Their answers would have broken your heart!

"I was born a Christian."

"My parents are Christian, that makes me a Christian."

"Just go to church and you're a Christian."

"It's something about feeling guilty about something or other. I don't know what you have to feel guilty about, but it's something or other, and if you feel guilty, you're a Christian."

"If you go around with Christians—it's something about fellowship that makes you a Christian."

"If you behave and lead a good life, you're a Christian."

Not one of the young persons sitting there knew how to become a Christian. Not one had ever been told that he must be "born again."

Not one knew about accepting Jesus Christ as Savior and Lord.

Not one knew that sinners have to be forgiven of their sins!

In a world where communication is present in all forms: radio, TV, telephone, newspapers, magazines, it broke my heart to realize that none of these young people had ever heard the communication of Christ.

About this time the lifeguard came up and was going to arrest me for "selling" on the beach without a license. I told him I wasn't selling anything. I was giving it away. One of the young men who originally had intended to roast me on a spit jumped up and said: "Take your hands off of her—she's telling us the most interesting things about the Bible we've ever heard."

The lifeguard unhanded me, and I whispered a prayer of thanksgiving to God.

I continued and the stillness of the beach was a surprising thing. I looked up and about twenty people were now listening. My cry went up to heaven as I said, "You do it, Lord, because I don't really know what I'm doing."

And the Lord of my life, as always, came through. I read the Four Spiritual Laws and eight young people nodded their heads in an acceptance prayer and a prayer of forgiveness.

I didn't drive back home after that—I just "floated home on a cloud."

I Find Witnessing Is Exciting
IN A HOSPITAL ROOM

One of the most thrilling conversions I ever witnessed occurred in a hospital room.

I had been asked to call on a man who was seriously ill in the hospital, and when I asked for information so I wouldn't go "blundering in," my pastor said, "Sometimes blundering is a blessing." I said, "Thanks a lot," little realizing the wisdom he had used.

Miami often has severe rainstorms and this was during the rainy season. That particular night it rained over eight inches. The highways were flooded; it took me twenty minutes to get from my office to a location which normally would take me three minutes. The water was completely over the highway, and it was pouring so hard it was impossible to see.

My night vision is not good, so I don't drive often at night. I wondered if the Lord wanted me to turn around and go back home to my nice, dry, warm house, and I asked him. I heard nothing, so I said, "Well, if You want me to go, You'll have to help me drive this car, and please, please prepare his heart for me as I make this long drive." Again I had asked God's Holy Spirit to go with me.

It took me two hours to drive what normally would have taken thirty minutes, and when I finally reached the hospital and parked the car, I stepped out into water nearly up to my knees. It was almost like a hurricane. I was soaked before I got two feet from the car.

My clothes stuck to me like glue (and I'm too fat to be good-looking in glued clothes), my shoes were ruined, my hair was dripping down in my face, and I'm sure I looked as far removed from an "Ambassador of Christ" as anyone could. I shivered as I entered the air-conditioned hospital (no wonder, I had accidentally gone into the morgue!), but after regrouping myself, I finally found the right room.

Three other men were in the ward, and as I talked a silence fell over the whole room. It was a thrilling moment because the Holy Spirit completely filled the room. Talking to the patient, I realized that God had prepared his heart and that he wanted Christ in his life. So I merely looked at him and said, "Would you like to accept Christ right now?" And then we prayed; first I prayed, and then for the first time in his life he prayed and asked God to forgive him for a lifetime of sins.

"Blundering was a blessing" in this case. Afterwards I was informed that this man had sneered at anyone who dared to mention Jesus Christ in his presence, but with God preparing his heart, my blundering was a blessing!

EVEN IN CHURCH

One of my greatest delights after winning someone to Christ is to watch that person grow and mature as a Christian. The Lord blessed whatever ministry I have by allowing me to be instrumental in leading my best friend to Christ.

In my B.C. (before Christ) days and D.L. (during liquor) days I spent a lot of time "martini-ing" with a couple whom I enjoyed very much. Shortly after meeting them, I became aware of the fact that for the tiny little person that she was, the wife could consume more alcohol than any person I had ever seen. And somehow or other she never showed the effects of one martini or ten. She never got drunk, or very seldom got drunk in the accepted sense of the word, but I often wondered how she could consume what she did without getting sick, or passing out, or something.

Her alcohol problem became increasingly worse over the years and I tried to caution her (as we drank martinis together) that she should cut down because it just wasn't good for her to drink so much. She's a very beautiful woman, with gorgeous, big brown eyes, and I warned her that if she continued to drink the way she was, it wouldn't be long before she wouldn't be pretty anymore, but this didn't seem to faze her. She went deeper and deeper into the bottle.

One time my friend's husband asked me to see what I could do about her alcohol problem because he had to go out of town for several weeks. I decided I would drink right with her, and then get her to stop before she was blotto! I failed to consider my own low tolerance for alcohol, and so before the week was out, she was still going strong, but I was completely baggy eyed and hung over. Then I decided to keep her so busy while her husband was away that she wouldn't have time to drink. Little did I know that after an evening of taking our children places, she would go home and spend the rest of the night drinking alone.

And then I found Christ! And when you first find Christ and your friends are not on that road, your friendship remains the same for a short while, but then the love for Christ overpowers everything else in your life and you discover you don't have anything in common with non-Christians.

Only once on the Christian road did I ever consider looking back. And that was for this friend. But when you really discover Jesus Christ, nothing is worth looking back for, and momentarily I regretted the fact that I had to leave her back there because I couldn't look back. There was only one way for me to go, and I knew it!

She continued to drink, and as she continued to drink, she watched the amazing change that was occurring in my life. She began to call me in the middle of the night and with a tiny little voice cry, "Help me, Frances, you've got to help me." I have talked for hours on the telephone trying to get her to leave the bottle alone, at anywhere from midnight to four o'clock in the morning.

She was attending a church halfheartedly where the gospel is apparently not preached, but in her groping for something she started the search which was to take her where she is today! She was intrigued with the way I was reading the Bible, so she dusted hers off, and started reading, too. But she only read in hers what she wanted to read. We have spent many hours on the midnight telephone discussing our different interpretations of the Bible.

The bottle became bigger and BIGGER and my heart really ached for her. I yearned to have her find the loving arms of Jesus Christ who could protect her from all harm. I had a reluctance to invite her to church with me, so I only went into ecstasy over what each Sunday did for me, hoping to make the claims of Christ sound so appealing that she would want to come with me one Sunday.

And then it happened!

One Sunday morning a little tiny hung-over voice called me and said, "Aren't you ever going to invite me to your church?" I could have cried! So I said, "Come today," and she said, "If I can pull myself together in time, I'll be there."

I went to Sunday school and didn't learn a thing that morning. All I did was pray! I prayed first that she would get there. Then I prayed that the minister would preach the kind of a sermon that would "grab" her, and then I prayed that God would open her heart so that she, too, could have the "abundant life."

God answered all of my prayers.

She got there all right! But she smelled so strong of whiskey she almost knocked me over. She apparently had had a "crying" jag because she showed the effects of weeping.

Second, my pastor must have preached just the right kind of sermon—or did God just use him in the right way?

Third, God cracked open the door of her heart. As in Sunday school, I didn't hear a word of the sermon, because I prayed the whole sermon through.

She returned the next Sunday after crawling in the bottle all week, only this time she didn't smell of alcohol.

She continued coming every Sunday and conversations concerning Christ became everyday occurrences, but the bottle became a bigger and bigger problem.

My pastor and I had prayed for her so much, because we saw a really lost soul, and because I loved her so much.

And then we had an evangelist for a week's revival at the church.

If anyone had told me two years prior to this that I would sit in church for eight nights straight, I would have told him he was off his rocker, but there I sat—eight nights in a row. I had given my friend a copy of the Four Spiritual Laws to read, and she came to several of the revival services. I could see that she was getting closer and closer to accepting Christ, and then one night during the invitation hymn, my pastor stepped down from his usual place in the pulpit. This put the three of us in a line—he was on one side of the room, she was in the middle, and I was on the other side. Somehow in that room she got caught in a crossfire of prayer between the pastor and me, and she turned to me and said, "Can't I be a Christian without accepting Christ?" I said, "Well, not hardly." She cut me off and said, "Oh, well, it doesn't make any difference," and stepped forward to accept Christ.

Being an emotional woman, I cried, because here was something I had prayed about for so long. She was now my sister in Christ.

I'm not going to tell you that all of her problems ended that night. Maturing as a Christian is sometimes a slow, tedious process. And I think God often tests us to prove our desires.

The alcohol still continued to be a problem, and she

tried to quit several times. Finally alcohol ceased to be a problem because it ceased to *be*, but this happened only after she finally yielded herself completely to Christ.

It is interesting how it finally happened. She had been invited to a cocktail party and didn't want to go because as she said, "You know I'm weak. . . . They'll offer me a drink and I'll take it, and when I take one, there I go again!"

I said, "When they offer you a drink, say 'No, thank you, I don't drink,' and before anyone can say a word, really get some prayers up to God asking him to back you up."

She has never touched another drop!

Today she is one of the strongest Christians I am privileged to know. And our Christian love is far greater than our "martini" love ever was.

Many people have asked me why I have such thrilling experiences as a Christian. If you haven't guessed the answer by now, let me tell you it's only because I allow Him to use me, and he will use YOU, too, if you will only let him.

CHAPTER 8

MY SPIRITUAL BRAINCHILD IS BORN

ONE of the burdens the Lord laid upon my heart early in my Christian experience was young people. As I watch the teen-agers of today with boys looking like girls and girls looking like boys, and all of them going down the sin path as fast as their feet can carry them, my heart cries out to help them.

A year or so ago I developed such a concern for young people who do not really know Christ in a personal way that I asked God to show me the way to make Christ a reality and a way of life to them. I looked at my own life and realized how much could have been accomplished had I had Christ on the throne of my life years ago. And I realized the waste of all those years.

I had seen a sign on a billboard which said, "I found how to get the most out of life after most of life was gone," and it slapped me right across the face as a true, but cutting statement about my own life. I thought of the old round of cocktail parties, dances, cigarettes, martinis, the desire to learn the latest dance steps. Recently I was horrified to read in a scrapbook that I had led in an exhibition of the "twist" at a radio broadcast.

So I began to pray.

And I prayed.

And I prayed.

And I prayed.

The summer came and was almost over when I made probably the greatest statement I've ever made in my life. I told my pastor he'd better start ducking. He knew I had been praying that God would show me the way to take Christianity to the kids in high school; he also knows when you ask God for a big request like that you'd better start ducking if you don't mean it, because He will really give it to you. I knew that God would give me the answer before school started, and so I knew there wasn't much time to back out if I didn't really mean it.

I prayed even harder.

One day a customer who is a wonderful Christian came into my office and I mentioned to him my prayers. Because the hand of God has human fingers many times, he picked up the telephone, made a call, and put me in contact with a man who has the same burden for young people that I do.

The net result of this was a frantic meeting (he drove some fifty miles to get to my house for a rush meeting, for the church youth camp started the next day). We almost talked the whole night through as we shared our ideas, and from this exciting meeting Alpha/Omega was born.

ALPHA/OMEGA

Alpha/Omega was to be a Christian youth movement to win others to Christ and to show them a wonderful "way of life." It was decided to take Alpha/Omega off the ground with a "Blast Off," program designed to appeal to young people. Because of this, I met two more of the "men in my life."

A big, good-looking football player from the University of Miami named Rick Strawbridge had been voted "the least likely to succeed on the Christian Road" a few months prior, but those who gave him this award had not reckoned how God was working in his life and how great was his decision and his dedication. Rick came into the office one day with Ed Waxer, and thus began another of the great loves in my life.

I asked Rick to give the story of his encounter with Jesus Christ at the Blast Off, and in the following weeks my admiration and love for another Christian grew. I learned how to establish rapport with teenagers through the willingness of this young man to share unselfishly of his time. Rick has been one of the strong arms of Alpha/Omega as it has floundered and then grown. So many young people have the idea that religion is for old "fuddy-duddies," and Rick really brought sparkle into it with his "P.T.L." (Praise the Lord). Few young people will ever come out and say,

71

"Praise the Lord," but we hear "P.T.L." said all the time.

At the beginning of the year a drama trio from Anderson College had performed at our church in a play called "The People Vs. Christ." A young man named Fred Clemens did an outstanding job of acting in this most unusual play. I got a chance to know him because I asked the trio to stay at my home. The next day I was giving a barbecue so the young people in the church could get a chance to know them and see these wonderful living examples of Christianity. This would prove that Christians really do lead the most exciting lives in the world.

We had such an exciting evening we forgot to go to bed. We were sharing all the fabulous Christian experiences we had all had, and at four-thirty in the morning I started the barbecue sauce for the party the next day. I'll never know how we made it to church on time, but we did! When I saw my pastor I flatly announced that I had a "Christianity hangover" from overindulgence. I will say this—I have had hangovers in my time, but this was the only one I ever enjoyed. And I have also spent many boring evenings in the most elegant of cocktail lounges, country clubs, and other places, but I have never spent a boring evening discussing Jesus Christ.

Now that I look back, it seems to me that most of the conversation centered on the word "saved." This word went against my grain from the word go and I guess it still does. I spent most of the night trying to convince Fred that it was much more acceptable and loving to ask someone to accept Christ instead of asking him to be "saved." The word grabbed me, and still does. During the twenty-four-hour period Fred spent at my house, I discovered what a wonderful Christian he is, and what a wonderful sense of humor he has.

So when the time came to think about who to use in the "Blast-Off" for Alpha/Omega, his name came to me. I wrote to him and asked him if he would do a comedy act poking fun at the unchristian acts of to-day's teen-agers. Since Fred was studying for the ministry, he was floored by my request and wrote that he would pray about it. In the final analysis I guess I outprayed him, for he came and did an outstanding and never-to-be-forgotten job.

The girl in the play was a charming young lady named Linda Cotton, and since I had lost her address, when I wrote Fred asking him to do the acting bit, I asked him if Linda would come along to sing.

Fred wrote back that Linda has a brother named Gene who he felt was really great and since they were going to be staying at my house, it would be easier for two fellows to stay than a fellow and a girl. So on blind faith I accepted Gene Cotton, another of the great loves of my life. Fred told me Gene was entertaining the troops in Vietnam, but would be back in time for the show.

Frantic preparations went on as we readied for the big show because I sure didn't know what I was doing—I had never been involved in anything like this.

The days grew closer and then one day the phone rang and it was Gene Cotton. He was in Atlanta changing planes and he would arrive in Miami two hours later.

I called my pastor and asked him to go with me because all of a sudden I panicked. I thought: What if I don't like him? . . . Can I be *sure* he's a Christian? . . . What if he's a lousy singer and what kind of a guitar player is he?

We drove to the airport, the flight arrived, and we waited while it unloaded. This was really "guitar players" day. About the first passenger off the plane was carrying a guitar (or a machine gun case) and my heart sank! Here was a bearded beatnik of the first degree.

I was afraid to look at him, so I died a thousand deaths before he rushed into the arms of a waiting female beatnik.

I breathed a little easier.

And then I saw another guitar case. This time I really flipped! What was carrying the guitar case would have scared anyone! I really prayed!

And the second guitar went by.

I decided I wasn't going to look anymore because I couldn't stand the strain. I would wait until someone asked me who I was.

Then the last guitar player came off the plane. And the Lord had introduced me to a brother in Christ who was to greatly influence my life, because we shared the same compelling drive in our miles-apart, years-apart, altogether different types of lives. But because of our mutual desire to show young people "His way of life," Gene Cotton and I joined hands in Alpha/Omega.

My Spiritual Brainchild Is Born
FOLK SINGING

From the very first meeting with Gene Cotton until the frantic "good-bye" after the Alpha/Omega Rally, the Lord continued to cross my path with this particular brother in Christ. Little did we realize at that time how the hand of God was working in bringing the abilities of two Christians together to further his kingdom.

When Gene accepted Christ, he rewrote the words of a familiar folk song entitled "I Can't Help But Wonder Where I'm Bound," changing it to "I No Longer Wonder Where I'm Bound." I have his permission to share his song in this book because it truly tells the story of all Christians.

*And I can't help but wonder where I'm bound, where
     I'm bound,
No, I can't help but wonder where I'm bound.
Well, once I led a life that was toil, sin, and strife,
Never thought that I would see the day
That I could look down without having to turn around.
But it's here, my Lord, and I know it's going to stay.
And I no longer wonder where I'm bound, where I'm
     bound,
No, I no longer wonder where I'm bound.*

*'Twas a life of sin and woe, and I hated to let it go,
But I heard a voice calling from above,
"If you'll but follow me, I'll give you life eternally,"
So I gave myself for everlasting love.
And I no longer wonder where I'm bound, where I'm
     bound,
No, I no longer wonder where I'm bound.*

*Now I've started on my way, and I live by Him each
     day,*

And I know in Him I always will abide.
And when I meet that Chosen One,
He'll say my job has been well done—
"Won't you come with me and sit down by my side?"
And I no longer wonder where I'm bound, where I'm
   bound,
No, I no longer wonder where I'm bound.

For me, life began at the cross of Calvary and the old road ended there, too.

One of the most unusual answers to prayers came as a result of mine and Gene's friendship and I always refer to this incident as "The Night the Lord Used a Cherry Pie."

During Gene's initial visit to Miami, I made a real gooey whipped-cream cherry pie. Gene immediately generated a very special "love" for this particular pie and on his subsequent visits to Miami I made one each night. During a phone call on my birthday he asked me if I thought I could make a pie and send it to him in Columbus, his hometown. I said "Sure." He said, "You're kidding. How could you get it to Columbus?"

My only comment was, "I'll make the pie; you ask the Lord to get it to you." We ended our conversation with my telling him the pie would be in Columbus two days later.

I flew to the store (I hope you will note I never walk, I always "fly") the next day and bought the ingredients and two metal pie tins to ship the pie in, and then I prayed. I said, "Lord, to strengthen the bonds of Christian love between my brother in Christ and me, will You please see that this pie gets to Columbus tomorrow?" (I hope you will note that I did not ask the Lord to get it there because I made the best cherry pie in the world, or because Gene liked the cherry pie, *but only to strengthen the bonds of Christian love.*)

And God answered that prayer. I picked up the telephone and called an acquaintance of mine who is a pilot and said, "Bob, I've got to get a whipped-cream cherry pie to Columbus tomorrow. Do you know anyone who flies the Columbus run?"

Now everyone calls up utter strangers, don't they, and asks them to fly a pie someplace or another for them? I asked as nonchalantly as if I were asking him to tell me what time it was, and he replied the same way—just as if it were a very ordinary everyday experience to fly whipped-cream pies—and said he didn't know anyone who flew the Columbus run.

BUT HE HADN'T RECKONED THAT GOD WAS WORKING IN THIS SITUATION! He called me back within a few minutes and said, "Fran, you'll never believe it, but the regular pilot on the Columbus run is sick, and my best friend has the run. Take the pie down there at four-thirty in the afternoon to his house and he'll be glad to take it for you." I just said "Thank You, Lord," took the pie down to the pilot's house, called Gene and told him to meet Pie Flight No. 304 arriving in Columbus at 9:05 and ask for the pie being carried special delivery. Gene later told me they really were looking for him at the Columbus airport when he picked up the pie because apparently some people just don't understand that it's possible for the Lord to charter a 727 jet to fly a pie

77

someplace for the sole purpose of strengthening bonds of Christian love. I'd like to give a special thanks to Eastern Airlines for unknowingly cooperating with the Lord.

CHAPTER 9

THE REAL MEANING OF CHRISTMAS

CHRISTMAS, 1966, became very special in my life, because it completed my first full year of being a Christian. Each year I had sent out a "Christmas" letter to all my friends, telling them of the events of the year: how many kittens the cat had, how we fared during the hurricane, and so forth. But Christmas took on a new dimension. I completely rebelled at the thought of sending out the usual "newsy" letter and so instead of the funny, frivolous Christmas letter I usually sent, the Lord laid upon my heart a letter telling what had happened in my own personal life.

And the interesting thing is, when the Lord lays a burden upon you there is no getting away from it (and neither is there any desire to get away from it), and so a *real* Christmas letter was written and sent to all my Christian and non-Christian friends. Even my Christian friends suggested that I should not send it because it was so definite in its meaning. They said, "People will think you're nuts." I said, "Great!" The following Christmas letter was the result.

1966
THIS WAS THE YEAR.....
OF OUR LORD

Each year we always have so much to tell, but this year we have a different message to bring.

The usual things happened . . .
. . . and the unusual happened.

I guess it really started last year when I had my eye operation. Looking back now, I realize this was probably the biggest blessing that ever happened to me, because it caused me to open my spiritual eyes and look things over. Much to my amazement, even though I had been brought up in church, I discovered that I really did not personally know Jesus Christ.

. . . And then I met Him
. . . and nothing changed
. . . "except my whole life."

My Bible which had been covered with dust for years, became the most inter-

esting book in the entire world . . .
and a thirst was created for knowl-
edge which I hope is never satisfied.

There's a verse in John which says:
"I am come that they might have life,
and might have it more abundantly." How
true! I always thought my life had been
very exciting, but never have I ex-
perienced such a fabulous life, and as
new doors open, I look forward to each
day with anticipation.

And to tell you about the excitement day
by day would take pages, so I'll sum it
up and say, "This was truly THE YEAR OF
OUR LORD."

To many of you who have read my Christmas
letters for years, this one may seem
strange. I hope you understand, because
my wish for you is the

    PEACE,

        JOY, and

           HAPPINESS

which fills your life when you know Him
personally.

                Frances

My family continues to be fine. Tom and Jan bought a new house this month. Joan continues to be the delight she has always been.

Never have I ever sent anything which had the impact of this simple message. Many people called to tell me it had made them stop and look at their own "Christianity" or "Churchanity" as some of them called it. Some wanted to know how they, too, could know Jesus Christ in a personal way.

And because I had found the true meaning of Christmas, I was compelled to put my thoughts into a play or monologue which was presented at our church. The young people sang the familiar Christmas carols, and when they had finished singing, all the lights were turned off with the exception of a blue spotlight which shone on a Christmas tree gaily decorated with tinsel and colored ornaments. I read the following offstage while all eyes were glued on the Christmas tree. (Note: The final song sung by the youth choir was "Deck the Halls with Boughs of Holly.")

HEAVEN'S CHRISTMAS TREE

"Deck the halls with boughs of holly."

How many of us have done just that during the past two weeks, only instead of decking the halls with boughs of holly, we have decorated spruce and pine trees with tinsel and ornaments, and lights and glitter. Probably most of you here tonight have Christmas

trees in your homes. . . . And sometime between tonight and tomorrow morning or tomorrow noon there
will be a time of giving and a time of receiving.

. . . a time of giving what?

. . . a time of receiving what?

Pretty packages? . . . clothes that don't fit? . . . shoes
that are too small or too big? . . . things for the house
that you don't really need? . . . things for you that you
don't really want? There will be many gifts ex-
changed this week, and some of them will be useful,
practical ones, some will be exciting and frivolous,
some will be expensive, some will be cheap.

As the thought persisted about the exchanging of
gifts, I seemed to be asking the Christ of Christmas
what kind of gifts are these, and the answer came from
the Scriptures: "And on either side of the river, was
there the tree of life" (Revelation 22:2).

Yes! *He* is the tree of life—the great Christmas tree
set up in this world, with presents for every creature
God has created. This means for the very poorest of
people. Those of you who have no one to make your
hearts glad with presents can turn to Jesus and find in
him a present just right for you. Lots of presents with
your name on them await you tonight under Heaven's
Christmas Tree.

Here is the first gift for you. (One of the youth
walked over and placed a beautifully wrapped package under the tree.) The GIFT OF LOVE. The pre-
cious, undying love of God. In John 3:16 the Bible
says, "For God so loved the world, that he gave his
only begotten Son, that whosoever believeth in him
should not perish, but have everlasting life."

Yes, the first package is a beautiful package, because it contains the GIFT OF LOVE. The Bible says, "Faith, hope, love abide, these three; but the greatest of these is love." God is giving to you his love. It is a gift with no strings attached. Will you accept the first gift?

Here is the second gift—the GIFT OF FORGIVE-NESS. Romans 3:23 says, "For all have sinned, and come short of the glory of God." And then Romans 6:23 says, "For the wages of sin is death." Man was created to have fellowship with God, but because of his own stubborn self-will, man chose to go his own independent way and fellowship with God was broken. But the GIFT OF FORGIVENESS shines with all the brilliance of the light of Christ's face, and yet it is stained bright red with the blood of Calvary. "Set in a frame carved out of the love of God, it dazzles like the chandelier of a thousand promises," yea, even a million promises.

The second gift is probably the most costly of all the gifts on Heaven's Christmas Tree. Do you see those fingerprints? They were left there by the nail-pierced hands of the Man of Galilee. Put there in the darkness and earthquake of that horrible afternoon when he took on the sins of all mankind.

There are many who need this gift. No one can say that he has never sinned against God. No one has ever had his sins wiped out by his own deeds. Everyone who has had his sins forgiven has had them forgiven through Jesus Christ. And just as others have been forgiven because of Jesus Christ, so everyone in this entire world can and may be forgiven of their sins. It can be done, now, this very night. This very special night when Christ was born. How many of you who are guilty of sin will take this package right now? The GIFT OF FORGIVENESS is yours—just for reaching out and accepting it. What will you do about this gift?

With the GIFT OF FORGIVENESS comes another gift, the GIFT OF PEACE—a perfect peace which floods your soul when you know you have accepted the GIFT OF LOVE and the GIFT OF FORGIVENESS. Philippians 4:7 says, "The peace of God . . . passeth all understanding." For many individuals the things of this world are so uncertain and so fleeting that they don't know whether or not tomorrow holds for them the same blessings they enjoy today. The friendships of earth sit on such slender, shaky, delicate pedestals and can be so easily knocked over that one is almost afraid to move, but the friendship of Jesus Christ is an undying one and with it comes peace—peace, wonderful peace.

God alone knows how many troubled and unhappy persons there are in the world tonight . . . how many there are in the city of Miami . . . how many are here in this very building . . . people who are troubled and have heavy hearts because they have not accepted the GIFT OF PEACE which comes from knowing Jesus Christ in a personal way.

No one will tell you that your troubles will all disappear when you become a Christian, but the gift of peace is a permanent possession of yours because Christ gives you a way to overcome your troubles and problems. Even the wonderful Apostle Paul com-

in the flesh, but he lived the
↗se he accepted the GIFT OF
was able to be an overcomer.

'T OF FREEDOM—a highly prized
gift. Joh. ↗ays, "You will know the truth, and the
truth will make you free." Psychiatrists say the
number one problem in the world today is guilt.
Christ will give you freedom from guilt because the
blood of Christ washes away your sins.

We live in a land where we say we have freedom,
but many people will go to bed tonight not really
knowing what freedom is because real freedom can
never come until Christ sits on the throne of one's life.
Then and only then will the individual know real
freedom. Romans 8:2 says, "For the law of the Spirit
of life in Christ Jesus has set me free from the law of
sin and death."

Here is your personal freedom. Will you accept it?

The next gift is the GIFT OF ABUNDANT LIFE.
The Bible says, "I am come that they might have life,
and that they might have it more abundantly." Yes,
this package is the GIFT OF ABUNDANT LIFE.

Webster defines abundance as: "a great plenty; an
overflowing quantity; ample sufficiency; fullness,
overflowing." As synonyms it gives: "plenteousness,
exuberance, plenty, plentifulness, riches, affluence, co-
piousness, wealth."

Think about these things—*a great plenty; an overflowing quantity*—when something overflows, it
means that you have more than you can hold; *ample
sufficiency*—again, who could possibly want more out
of life than an ample sufficiency; *fullness, overflow-*

ing—imagine your cup of life filled to the top and overflowing with the riches of Christ.

If I told you that inside of this box there is a million dollars for anyone who would dare to reach out and take it, what would you do? Would you reach out and take it?

Would you know that this was the overflowing quantity—the ample sufficiency—the fullness—the overflowing—that Christ promised? I'm sure that if you knew that inside that box was a cashier's check for one million dollars, you'd all rush right up here to grab it.

But what if I told you that the gift inside this box is far greater than anything money could buy? Would you take it? This is the gift that is worth *more* than a million dollars—the GIFT OF ABUNDANT LIFE. *Your* name is on it—do you want it? Will you accept it?

This last gift is shining like a million lights or a billion stars, and is glittering so beautifully that you can either close your eyes because the light is so bright, or you can see it through the eyes of faith. The last package contains the GIFT OF ETERNAL LIFE. John 1:12 says, "But as many as received him, to them gave he power to become the sons of God, even to them that believe on his name."

Not only do you have the GIFT OF ABUNDANT LIFE *now*—you also have the GIFT OF ETERNAL LIFE. The span of life which we live on this earth is so minute compared to all eternity, but this is what you are being given under Heaven's Christmas Tree tonight.

Christ says, "I am the Way, the Truth, and the Life: no man cometh unto the Father, but by me." He didn't say, "I am A way, A truth, and A life." He said, "I am THE way, THE truth, and THE life." And that life is eternal life.

Look at all the packages under the tree, and examine their contents:

THE GIFT OF LOVE

THE GIFT OF FORGIVENESS

THE GIFT OF PEACE

THE GIFT OF FREEDOM

THE GIFT OF ABUNDANT LIFE

THE GIFT OF ETERNAL LIFE

Think about the packages under your Christmas tree tonight. Are you waiting to open any packages which will compare with the gifts under Heaven's Christmas Tree? Could there possibly be any package under your tree, regardless of how expensive, how big, how small, how luxurious, or how cheap, that can compare with these gifts which are being offered to you tonight?

But a gift is not a gift until it is accepted; everything is right here for you to accept.

Will you make this the most notable Christmas of your life because you have found what Christmas really is, because you have found that Christmas is Christ?

There are the gifts:

LOVE

FORGIVENESS

PEACE

FREEDOM

ABUNDANT LIFE

ETERNAL LIFE

As Gene Cotton sings "O Holy Night," will you come and accept these gifts, which are all yours from Heaven's Christmas Tree, and let the Light shine in your life? or will you turn away to remain in darkness?

Let's change the words to "Oh holy night, O night when *I* was born." You, too, can have the same birthday as Christ, just by accepting his gifts right now.

(Note: When reading the paragraph which states "and let the Light shine in your life," every light was flashed on. When reading, "Or will you turn away to remain in darkness?" the lights went off again. Also as each gift was mentioned, a beautifully wrapped package was placed under the tree.)

CHAPTER 10

GOD'S PLAN FOR MY LIFE

AS I write this final chapter of the now saved "unsaved" Christian, I remember the words in the Book of Psalms: "Be still, and know that I am God."

My life has been so enriched and so full since I finally became totally bound to Him that I have often felt I would actually burst right out of my physical self.

There came a plus into my life the day that Christ first reigned supreme, and that "plus" has been there ever since. For one brief fleeting moment I wondered if it was worth losing my friends for, but the moment was so fleeting I don't hardly remember anymore that it ever existed. And the plus sign in my life is the cross of Christ.

I publicly announced on my fiftieth birthday that I had hardly been able to wait for the fabulous fifties.

Because my fiftieth year was really my first complete "Year of our Lord" it was the most fabulous year of my life. I recently saw my fifty-first birthday and Alpha/Omega surprised me with an unbelievable birthday party. I expect my fifty-first year to be even more fabulous than my fiftieth. . . . And just wait until I hit the spiritual sixties!

Christianity is a state of being—a way of life! And if I have painted the abundant life in glowing terms, I meant to, because there's nothing that compares with it. As I mentioned previously, the biggest sin in the world today is the sin of compromise. And this is the sin which keeps many from living the abundant life.

Don't mess around with Jesus if you don't mean it, because he doesn't want just a part of you. The Lord of my life is really selfish—he isn't satisfied with just part of me—He wants *all* of me, just like he wants *all* of you. And it's a funny thing—once you have tasted Christ, nothing else satisfies. I'll guarantee you, if you really step out on faith the first time, try as you may, you will never be able to go back, because Jesus won't "mess around with you." When he takes you completely and positively because you yield yourself to him, he brands you with a brand that burns to the very core of your being.

The abundant life gives me a life that allows me to rise above every crisis that may come along in the "worldly world" because "I am *in* the world, but not *of* the world." Only those who actually experience this can ever understand.

Christianity and the abundant life are not a series of mountains and valleys to me—rather they form a plateau which allows me to stay at an even level all the time. And I feel that the more complete and total a person's dedication, the higher the level of his plateau.

If you want to be miserable, give Christ a *little* slice of your life. Sometimes I feel people are much better off who don't even bother going to church if that's the extent of their Christianity. I remember years ago saying, "I don't want to go to heaven because I want to be where all my friends are." The amazing thing today is I'm sure there are going to be far less people in heaven than any of us imagine because the Bible says, "Many are called, but *few* are chosen." Every person in this wonderful land we live in has the opportunity to hear the words of Christ. So many are called, but how many of them actually fail to heed the call of Christ, and therefore cannot be chosen.

I do not know yet what God wants out of my life. I only know that each day I let him know that I am available for whatever purpose he has for me. And it's a peculiar thing, it doesn't really make any difference what he shows me now that I am waiting on him, because since I asked Christ to live his life through me, what *I* do is inconsequential, but I'm really eager to see what he's going to do!

And to find out, I'm going to keep on saying every morning, "Lord, what fabulous things are we going to do today?"